From The Streets

To The Pulpit

Mark L. Brown

From The Street To The Pulpit

©2015 Mark Brown.

All Rights Reserved.
Published by KCM Publishing 2015

No part of this book may be reproduced, stored in a retrieval system or transmitted by any means without written permission from the publisher except for brief quotations in critical reviews or articles. Unless otherwise noted Scripture quotations are from the New King James Version. Used by Permission. Scripture quotations marked ASV are from the American Standard Bible Copyright. Scripture quotations marked HCSB are from the Holman Christian Standard Bible. Scripture quotations marked AMP are from The Amplified Bible Copyright © 1954, 1958, 1962, 1964, 1965, 1987 by The Lockman Foundation. All Rights Reserved. Used by Permission.

Dedication

I want to thank my Lord and Savior, Jesus Christ. You rescued me from destruction and devastation and are truly a restorer. I would be nothing, without you.

A special thanks to my beautiful wife. I love you and am grateful for your support of my vision.

Introduction

This story is about a young man that was in the streets of Cleveland and God came and changed his life. Mark is going to tell you about life experiences, with the streets and also with death. This book is basically about his life and it is a true story. While reading this book, I am praying that your life will be changed and you will turn completely to God. My goal for writing this book is not for fame. I really want God to get all the glory, out of this book. I want to thank everyone for reading my personal story, **"From The Streets To The Pulpit."**

From The Street To The Pulpit

Table of Contents

Chapter One: How It All Started..6

Chapter Two: High School Days..12

Chapter Three: Summer Time Fun..16

Chapter Four: Back On My Home Turf..20

Chapter Five: I Thought I Kew It All..25

Chapter Six: A Turn Around The Wrong Corner............................31

Chapter Seven: Welcome To The Real World............................35

Chapter Eight: God Is Speaking..45

Chapter Nine: Family Life..53

Chapter One

How It All Started

It was a cold November night, in 1992, when I first started seeing drugs and stealing them, from my father. He use to have so much, he wouldn't have known it was gone. He never found out I took them either. I told my brother I wanted to be a drug dealer. I was sitting at the table, with my family and he told my parents. They immediately got on me and stated that I was going to be dead or in jail. My father was really pissed off. He was in his mad mode.

God was calling me then, but I wasn't listening. He showed me the end of the world, in a dream. In the dream, I saw a serpent, on one side, and the great day on the other side of the house. The Bible says it is going to be a great and terrible day. Back to the dream, God had brought His hand down and I got in it and went up with Him and then I woke up. This dream scared me for a minute, but I went back to the hustle.

I done had heard the speech and had this dream, but I wanted to do what I wanted to do. My grandfather died. Elder Irving Brown was a true man of God. I would see demons tremble, when he walked past. I saw him cast out devils, with no problem. I was very sad, because six months earlier my other granddaddy died. I was at a loss for words. My mother and aunties were going through and were very sad. I wanted to change then, but the devil had my mind. He wanted me to go sell drugs and be in a gang. Now the end of the year was approaching and I had in my mind as to what I was going to do on New Year's Eve. I was young, but had a mind of a grown up. I was thinking ahead. I was thinking I am about to be 13 years old and going to have sex, for the first time. I was getting my money. I was getting girls, but still managed to have good grades. I was still on the merit roll, but as usual stayed, in the streets. I was sitting at home watching my little brother and heard a loud noise hit the house. I thought was an earthquake in Cleveland, not knowing that it was a bull dozer hitting up against house.

My dad had come home and was angry. Thank God, I was able to stop him and it. It was almost in the basement, but God stopped it.

My mom was in the newspaper, the next day, looking shocked at the hole that was in the side of the house. It was hard for me because, I wanted to know who did this to us. I was going to find out one way or another.

I gathered some of my friends at school and we started putting our eyes and ears to the streets. We found out who did it. It was a boy from my school. I definitely had to beat him up and my friends did too. We gave him the business. He said he was sorry, but he could have killed my family. I went home and told my dad and mom what happened and they didn't press charges, though they should have. I was mad, because we had to use the bath room outside. It was an outhouse. We had to take showers at my grandmother's house. I had started to live with my grandmother, because she was alone since my grandfather had died. I started to see myself at school and was not interested. In 1993, I started to think I was grown and began to support myself.

I had become good at lying. I still played football, because that was the one thing to keep me out of trouble. My father was the coach, so I really didn't have a choice. I still didn't see the call on my life.

From The Street To The Pulpit

I had a call since birth and the anointing was on my life. Things started to change, when I moved from Kinsman to Garfield on 131st. I had to meet new friends and learn a lot of new things. I went from Nathan Hale to AB Hart and the kids were bigger and looked older. I had to ride the bus and there were a lot of things happening on the bus.

The bus ride was off the chain with fights, windows busted out and people not listening to the bus driver. I was in that crowd myself and was doing stuff, just because. I was always going to school, in the best clothes and shoes. Jordan's were my favorite shoes. I really didn't want another shoe to wear. My family had to have them.

I have another sister and she only visited on vacations and holidays. I grew up in a great home, well-mannered, but wanted to try other options. We as people try stuff, even if it's good or bad. It's in our nature. A little time in my new school I got my first F, on my report card.

I had never gotten an F knew and when I got home I knew it was over. My mom was going off at first, but she said, "Son, I know you can do better."

I went to school the next day and it got worse. I bought some weed from my neighbor and tried to sell it. I was selling cocaine, at first. It was time for me to try another drug game. I was doing it for a while, until I got caught. It was my birthday. I tried to show my mother how much money I made by the kids giving me money at school and the weed fell out.

The first thing she said was what you are doing with that. I told her I found it. She said that I was lying and she was telling my father. She told me to go to my room. I was like a typical kid thinking of what he was going to do to me. I was pacing the floor and I could have made a hole in it. I heard the car pulling up and felt my stomach do something I never felt before. I ran down the stairs, before mom told him. I didn't want her to add extra to the story. Dad came into the house and mom told him what she had found. He asked me where I got the weed from and I lied. I told him I found it on the way to school.

I couldn't get anything past him. He was like a detective and interrogate me. He told me if I didn't tell him he was going to whoop me. His voice raised and he asked me again, so I told him it was from the boy across the street.

He asked if I was smoking it too and I said yes. He called the across the street and we were sitting, at the table.

I was glad he didn't tell their mother. My neighbors were so mad at me that they didn't talk to me for a while. That passed over and it was near the end of the school year. I was about to graduate from the 8th grade. Summer came and it was time for me to sell drugs full time. I was selling weed all summer long. I even got my first piece of sex. You couldn't really tell me anything. She was 18yrs old. I always liked older women and I was only 13yrs old, even then I was still in shock. I wasn't wet behind the ears anymore, like the old folks would say.

Chapter Two

High School Days

The fall came and I went to John Adams High School. You know the first day of school that I had to be fresh. I even started high school football, because I was too big for little league football. I went to practice every day. One thing about football, I never sat the bench. I was always a leader and not a follower. John Adams was so special to me, because my mother and father graduated from there.

The people I grew up with all went to this school. It was crazy that they had to check for guns, knives, drugs, pagers and also cell phones. I got a lot of pagers taken from me. The gang task force was up at the school every day. I was doing well at first and still passing my classes school was my motivation, besides football. The football season was going good, until I broke both of my ankles. I thought my career was over. My team mates were very upset, when I got hurt.

From The Street To The Pulpit

The football coach was angry that he had to put someone, in my spot that wasn't as good as me. I had to train him and teach how to play the position. I was out 3-4 weeks and was so mad, because I wanted to play. I loved the game. I came back right, before the JV championship game. I had to let you all know that I played Varsity and JV in the 9th grade and was in beast mode. The big game was coming up and we were playing our rivalry John F Kennedy. Before we went to the championship, they were in our way. The game had started and I remember sacking the quarterback. He was my friend. I also remember us kicking the ball off and I ran down the field and tried to tackle this guy. I missed and I had got up and ran and tackled him under the bench. God bless my friend (Antwan "Sleepy" Kirkman). I hit him so hard that he came over to my house after the game wanted to fight me. I didn't know, until I got home and the kids in the neighborhood told me. This was one of the best games of my life and we won. We went undefeated that year. The next week we were going to the championship to play East High.

We get to the game and the boys were so big they looked like the varsity team. We as a team were happy to get to the championship and didn't care who was there were.

We were going to beat them. One thing I enjoyed as a kid and about high school was winning championships. We won the game and the coach was so happy. Now the season was over it was the middle of the school year. I was 14yrs old with not a lot going on, but getting detentions every day. I was the class clown or just had to make people laugh all the time. We got wind that our school was closing and the whole school was upset. We all were wondering what school we were going to. My dreams were killed I was not going to graduate from my mom and dad's high school. The school year was going on and people weren't the same. The only thing kept people together were the basketball games. I loved them because, they were always crowed and I had the new Jordan on basically every time they came out, during the season. People thought I was on the team, but I wasn't. I had the skills, but didn't like the uniforms they had. They were too tight.

I hung out with the players and that's why they thought I was on the team. My mom would meet me at the games and bring me the shoes, all the time. I remember I snuck out of town to Chicago to get shoes. I was hanging with the wrong crowd and my parents didn't even know. I can talk about it now, because it is over and done with.

My circle of friends was tight. It was Bubba, Tee, Dame, Rell and my brother. The school year was ending again. People were doing whatever, since the school was closing. They were throwing stuff at the teachers and fighting too. I didn't go to school, on the last day. The people who graduated and the alumni's were all up there. It was a sad day and people were crying. I was getting ready for the summer again and I wasn't really ready for that, but selling drugs was on my mind. My focus had gone in a whole different direction. Money had my attention.

Chapter Three

Summer Time Fun

It was a great summer and my friends and I were hanging out on the corners selling drugs and doing our thing. We had the best dope in Cleveland and it made us a lot of money. Money was rolling in and I thought this was the good life. Having a pocket full of money was the thing. You know money, women and driving cars was very enticing. I am going to share my spring break of 1995. My older friend who was about 20 years old told me to get in the car with him. He told me we were going to Atlanta. I had just gotten my work permit. I was thinking about finding a job. We he said we were going to the Freak Neek and I said let's go. My parents didn't know. Once again, I told them I was spending the night over at my friends' house. God was covering me and I didn't even know it then. We went down here and it seemed anything goes. In Atlanta, there were women who cost from $50.00 to $500.00 at the time selling sex. I was so amazed about this. I didn't have to worry about anything, because my OG had me covered.

I ate good, smoked good and had women that cost me $300.00. It felt like one of the craziest and best times, of my life. We were there 3-4 days. Now it was back to reality, in Cleveland Ohio. I had went back to school and was telling people what I had done for Spring Break. They were amazed and said I was so young doing grown man stuff.

It was June and time for the summer vacation. My family wanted to go on a road trip and I was so mad, because they going to mess up my drug selling. My life was about to get crazy. We were down there for about a week. It was the worst week of my life and I never want go back there. My cousin wanted us to go to the jook joint and hang out. The boys, in this place, knew we were not from down here, so they wanted to start a fight. We were dancing with the girls and they didn't like that. Anyone who knows me knew I wanted to fight, but didn't know how many of them there were.

I had let them slide this time, as much as I didn't want too. My uncle and father were at this lady's house fixing a door and the boys came down there. They had bats, sticks, logs to fight with. We didn't even know what was going on. The boys had this army jeep riding past us and were playing I got five on it.

My dad and uncle followed them and saw it was us they wanted to fight and had stopped it. We got home that night and my uncle didn't want to turn on the air conditioner and it was a 100 degrees outside. I was ready to go home. He woke me up at about 11:00 pm to go outside and take the trash out. I told him no. He said you had to burn it and there was nothing but woods, behind the house. I didn't know what was in there. I told him no once again and went to lay back down. I went to bed and was as hot as hell, sweating like a mule. I woke up the next morning at about 5 am to run a mile, because I was going miss football practice for about a week. I had said, "Lord, if its 80 degrees this early in the morning, what it going to be later?" It was 102 degrees that day. They told us we were going to the beach, so we went on a road trip to get there.

We got to the beach and there was no one there, but us and the beach. Eventually, some people came and I had started to worry if we were in the wrong place. I remembered swimming and they had a sign in the middle of the lake saying do not pass this line with a fish on it. My brother and I had passed the line. Fish jumped out that water and you saw everybody running like little rascals.

From The Street To The Pulpit

We all laughed once we got on the land, because we never saw each other run like that. I had to talk about this trip, because this was one of funniest road trips we ever had.

Still in Alabama, we had saw history where the slaves use to live. We saw the cotton fields and where Martin Luther King marched at. I couldn't have been a slave. Men that picked cotton were paid so little and they had to pick it with thorns all around. Alabama was too country for me. My cousin had made this cake and it was so good, all homemade. She put her foot in that cake, as they would say. Now, we were packing about to go back to Cleveland. Thank you, Jesus.

Chapter Four

Back On My Home Turf

When I got back home to Cleveland, it was back on the streets for me and I couldn't wait. It was the end of the summer and now back to football practice. I knew that I going to be on the block after practice to about 12 midnight every night, until school started. I had to get together, because school was approaching and you know I had to be fresh, no doubt. My brother and I had ask my grandmother, if we could have a back to school party. My grandmother said yes, because she was cool like that. We planned a big back to school party. We went to all the neighborhoods we knew people and told them about it. They were so excited. We said we were going to charge $1.00 to get in and they could have all the food and pop they wanted. My grandmother's husband bought us a gallon of liquor for the party. I was 15 years old and my grandmother told me that I could drink. You know me and I was going to do it. I was the first grandchild, so my grandmother would always call me her baby. I had my whole crew at the party and we were getting it in too.

From The Street To The Pulpit

We had a good time, but you know someone was bound to start a fight. I had to get my cousin to be security, so we could enjoy ourselves. There were about 60 people in this back yard having the time of their life. I really was happy we pulled it off again. The next day, after the party, I heard some bad news. One of my crew members was in a bad car accident and was in critical condition. I cried all night long. He was older than me, but taught me the game. My friend, Tyrone Cason, was a hustler. He didn't bother anyone. But, if you bothered him, he would give you the business. He would do all night flights, for a whole week. He was about that money. We use to call him donkey knots, because he kept 3 or 4 rolls of money, on him. I found out what had happened to him and me and the crew went to look for the guy that bothered him. He was nowhere in sight. It was good that God was not letting us find this boy. We were thinking about doing all kinds of stuff to him. A couple of weeks had passed and the family decided to pull the plug, on him. He had been on life support. Because of the attack, he was a vegetable and nothing else could be done for him. I was mad I couldn't make the funeral, of my crew member. I had football practice and my coach was tripping, as usual.

He said if I went to the funeral, I wasn't going to play in the game that week. I knew Tyrone wasn't mad, because he loved football. He wanted me to be a star in football and not the streets. The school were in shock, when he died. I was at John F. Kennedy now. This was a new school. The kids from this school did not like John Adams kids. This school was so crowded at lunch the boys had to eat with the boys and the girls with the girls. I ate with all the young drug dealers, around the city. We had go to the gym to wait for when it was our time to eat and it was off the hook. You had people shooting dice, boxing, playing cards, 3 card molly and selling drugs. Everything was going down. It seemed like there was a Kinsman vs. Harvard fight every day. I was always crazy. I had to go to class, every day. I really had to keep my grades up to play football. One afternoon, I remember somebody coming to get me from class. They said my cousin Venus was fighting outside. I went out there just to make sure no guys jumped on her or tried to do something they would regret. This fight made me late for football practice. The coach was mad at me and I just couldn't wait for the season to end.

From The Street To The Pulpit

When the season was over I was cutting school, with my crew to go over to my girl's house to drink and smoke. We would smoke weed, sleep with the girls and then go back to the school house. Every day my dad dropped us off, at the library, right by the school and I wouldn't go in at first. I would sell my weed until it was all gone, then go into the school. I smoked, before I went in every day. I felt like I had to. The kids in the school would say he is always high. I was living in Garfield, so the kids would call me an OPH hustler, but I wasn't. I wasn't one of them. I am 108TH family, for life. I lived on Kinsman, for a while. I was a county nigga, for a minute. OPH means Open Pantry Hustler. They nicknamed people this, because they hustled at Open Pantry on 131st. I was about to turn the big 16 on January, 26, 1996 and I had a skating party on the Westside, at the USA skating rink. I had wanted a car for my birthday and didn't see it. I was so mad I could have hurt somebody. My whole family came out and all of my friends. We had a great time that night. The next day, I had got a job at McDonald's. This was my first job. My cousin worked there and got me the job. There were some fine girls that worked here. I had to get me one. You guys know what I'm talking about. I had a few of them liking me, because I was the new guy, I guess.

Things were going well, at the time a job. I was hustling, meeting girls and I was also losing weight. They couldn't tell me anything, once again. I went to work, but had to get that drug money too. I was buying more shoes and clothes, than ever. I had haters all around me and that came with the territory. Eventually, everything was coming together for me. It was spring break and I had to keep up with the latest shoes, even though we didn't have school. While on spring break, I got into a fight with this boy. I had to beat him half to death. I had a problem. My brother and I was always fighting guys. That was our trade mark. We would jump somebody, in a minute. Don't mess with the Brown brothers, they use to say. My brother and I looked like twins, so the girls thought we were each other, at times.

Chapter Five

I Thought I Knew It All

There was a lot of madness, at the school. I was back, in my routine, selling weed, smoking and kicking it. I was ready to drop out of school, but mom said, "If you drop out, you have to get out." She said that she didn't raise any drop outs or quitters. In this time, my mom and dad were very into church. They both stayed on me, but I wasn't listening. It was going in one ear and out the other. A couple of months past and it was the end of the school year. I got caught playing around, in the hallways. They told me if they catch me again, I was going to be suspended to the next school year. I didn't care, because I was ready to get out anyway. They said don't come back, until August and it was the end of May. I couldn't let my parents know, so I still got dropped off. I just didn't go into the school. I went to the cut spot. If I would tell you everything, I would have to kill you. You know you have to go to the grave with some stuff. Some things are between you and God. I started to hang with my neighbors, across the street from my mom's house.

Their names were Rashad, Rashada and Mike. They will be my brothers and sister, for life. Their mom and my mom were very cool with each. They started going bowling on Tuesdays and we decided to make it Tuesday night gambling over at their house. We couldn't wait for Tuesdays, so they could go bowling. They would have all the dope boys from Garfield and other places come over to gamble. I use to be over there and would lose my whole check and what I made that day, on the block. So, I would go back to the block to make some money and come back. I was not still caring that God was calling me. I was in church, but not feeling this was what I wanted to do. God was looking at me, but I wasn't looking at Him. I was about to get a new car. It was a 1980 regal. My grandmother's husband bought it for me, but I didn't have a license. So, you know I couldn't drive. My mom had to pay for me to go to Driver's Ed at Sears in Randall Mall. This was the most boring class and it cost her $175.00. I went to class, but on break I would go to the mall. Sometimes, I didn't go back and was really wasting my mother's money.

From The Street To The Pulpit

There were so many girls in this class. I use to keep it real with them. I wanted just sex. I didn't want a relationship. I didn't finish the class and my mom was so disappointed in me. I told her I was so sorry and she told me that I would not be driving. She was the one letting me drive. She was humble lady, all her life. "No license, no driving", she said, again. It was cool to me, because I was getting crack head cars. For those who don't know those are people who use drugs. My mom thought she was stopping something. She never knew that I had these folk's cars. I was going back to the streets and Maplerow Ave was the street that I really hustled on. We use call it the row or death row. I remembered they robbed a girl on the street and didn't care who you were. We played basketball, football, any bounce and baseball on the row. The row is the street we used to be on. There were a lot fights and gambling, on the row. My father use to also play with us, on the street. He was called Coach Mark. I used to sneak up on Miles Ave to make some money, in front of Miles Supermarket. I had friends everywhere, in Cleveland, Ohio.

Now, it was time to head back to this football practice. I liked to play football, but hated to practice. Some of the good players had graduated, but we still had an alright team.

I was on the varsity team and junior varsity wasn't for me. I was too advanced, for that. We started 2 a days. I was really pissed, because I had to work after practice, sometimes. I liked some of my team mates, but the others were so lame to me. My coaches stayed on me. I didn't know why. They saw something in me that I didn't see. One day, at the 2 day practice, we went to Finast got food in the back and didn't pay, in the front. I am telling you this, because I started doing this every day. I was stealing food. I knew better and still did bad. God was watching me and writing all this down. I didn't even care about it either. It was time to get my school paper to see what grade I was in. It said the 10th grade again. This couldn't be right. My mom ask me about it and I said they made a mistake. But, I knew I wasn't doing any work, in school. I was lying my butt off, to my mom. I went to football practice and the coach asked me the same thing. I just lied and said they had made an error or something. I was a good liar back then. The school year was starting again I was in the 10th grade, with 11th grade classes. I wasn't a dummy. I went down to the guidance counselor and asked what I had to do to get put, in my right grade. She said I had to do well and get good grades. They would put me up in January.

I was going on about my business and I had to do my work. I even pay some teachers, to get good grades. My school, JFK was off the hook. It was becoming like the movie, "Lean on Me." People were doing whatever. Fights and gambling was the norm. It seemed like it was anything goes. We had this principal Ms. Rice and she was the version of Joe Clark. She came to clean the school up. She had a drug list and if you were 18yrs old and not doing anything, she was kicking you out the school. She didn't play, at all. She was having people's lockers raided every day and you didn't even know until they called your name on the PA system. Everyone could hear. They started to get medal protectors too. She use to ride through the blocks to see if you were a drug dealer and if she saw you she would write your name down. She was taking the school back. A lot of kids loved her. She knew me and my brother personally and called us the Brown brothers. We were always coming to school late and always smelling like weed. I sold it, so we always had it. She use to say I smell you guys. Now, go to lock out. I use to be mad, because I hated going there. The lockout room was dirty, with a bunch of desks. We would sit there doing nothing, but looking in and out the windows sometimes.

I remember one day getting dropped off at school and they had metal detectors and police everywhere. I had to hide the weed, behind the dumpster and went in the school. I went back out there at lunch time and it was gone. I was so mad, but I didn't get caught with it. The school year went along and I got promoted to the right grade, in January. I was so happy. They told me I still had to go to summer school. It cost $100.00 to go, but it was no problem.

Chapter Six

A Turn Around the Wrong Corner

The summer time is here and people were getting ready for summer school, at South High. There were people from every school, basically from this side of town. These were people I knew from other folks. They knew I had the weed too, just like regular school. I stayed in front of the school to sell weed, before class. Summer school was easy and I passed with flying colors. God was about to save my life again and I didn't even realize it. One day on the way to summer school, my dad and I were in the car and my dad fell asleep at the wheel, while I was asleep. I woke up, right before we hit a pole and took the wheel. My dad woke up and said you better thank God for saving us. I have more testimonies, further into the book.

I finally made it to 12th grade, but still have to pass the math proficiency test. I was worried about that. I was focused on getting a scholarship in football. But, you know I still wanted to sell drugs. My mind was on playing football and finishing school.

I also wanted to sell weed and upgrade to selling cocaine rocks. I remember playing Bay Village High School. I caught an interception and ran a 50 yard touchdown. I was so happy, because that was my first touchdown, in high school. We were coming back, but we still lost the game. The season was still going on and I pulled my shoulder out of place, so I had to sit out some games. I was running for homecoming king too. I was selling tickets to whomever grown to win the competition. I had come back to practice, the week before homecoming. I had to get my car running, so I could drive to homecoming. On homecoming day, we had a ceremony at Kennedy to tell who won what. I won homecoming king! My parents and friends were happy for me and I can't leave out the football team. Now, the girls were really looking at me. The John Adams people were happy for me too. Its homecoming night and we won the game and it was time to get high and drunk. We partied all night long.

Everything was going smooth, until the math test came again. They were going to tell us the results. Once again, I didn't pass. I was sick. I started focusing on prom. It was the next big thing. My mom, dad and grandmother helped me with it.

I had a 98 Deville Cadillac and I was looking good. My date was looking good, but didn't get any from her and I was mad. It was close to the end of the year and I had to find out, if I passed, so I could graduate. My name was almost first. I was so happy to get to walk across the stage. I was so happy and my parents were proud of their son. My aunt and cousins came in from out of town, because my uncle got married right before I graduated. On the wedding day, my family and I got drunk and high. We had enough liquor that I took some home. On my graduation day, I still hung over, so took the liquor with me to share with some classmates. We were drinking and had a great time. I graduated and just couldn't believe it. I was mad afterwards, because my family didn't wait for me like every other parent and family did. I was being selfish.

Chapter Seven

Welcome to the Real World

It was two years after my graduation and selling drugs was a full time job. I moved out with my cousin Donnie and his wife in garden valley. I never lived in the projects before and it was a different life. I remember my mom gave me $20 and I bought some weed, by the end of the week I had $200. My cousin was helping me out. My parents didn't want me down there, because it was so dangerous. They were praying like crazy. There was so much going on down here. You had different parking lots with drugs. There were black men everywhere and females all over the place. There were guys called jack boys or robbers down here. I wasn't afraid, but they were wondering who I was. I was new and down here, every day selling weed. I was waiting on a customer one evening and saw the most terrible thing, in my life. I saw a man get his brains blown out for $66.00. I heard the whole thing. The man was a working man, with kids. When I saw that, I couldn't sleep for a couple of months.

I had continued to sell weed outside, with the old school guys. We use to take turns. After 3 o'clock, the young boys out there were too much for me. My cousin and I would come in the house, when they came out. I had started to smoke PCP and it started to get crazy. PCP is a dangerous drug. My cousin friend brought a whole ounce of it to sell and my cousin's wife was mad. The jack boys found out came over to ask if we had it. They were planning to rob us. We went and got guns to protect ourselves. We had shifts me. My cousin would take the day and I had the night. I had a shot gun and he had a 9mm. We were ready. My cousin and his wife would argue about me being there. I didn't like that. She would smile in my face, smoke my weed and then talk about me, behind my back. I couldn't believe it. The jack boys tried to rob my cousin one night and he shot one of them and they knew after that he was not playing. I was gambling and smoking, more than ever. I decided to go back to my mom and dad's house for a few days. My first day back in the hood and I had to fight a fool. This guy came to my mom's house to fight my brother, but I told him he had to fight me. I told him I was going to meet him, at the corner of my street.

I went down here and beat the brakes off him. A lot of people around never saw me fight, but after that I had no problems. The girls were out there and you know I couldn't lose the fight. I went back, to my project life. I had started to meet folks down here. I was back to the grind. People were getting killed left and right and anytime it could have been me. My dad use to come down here to pray for me and my cousin, all the time. He would pray, until God got me out of there.

Now it's 2002 and I was going to work and selling dope every day. I had got a crack head truck one day and went to jail. His wife called the truck in as stolen. I got caught coming from the club. I was mad, because they tried me as receiving stolen property and hanging with minors. We had weed, drinks and everything in this truck. I had cocaine rocks and had to put it where police didn't find it. I was in the jail downtown for the first time. The first person to see me was my friend and best friend, Stacy's mom. I had just been over to her house about a week before. I was ashamed. I knew not to call home, because my father was going to say I told you so. I didn't want hear that, at the time. He prophesied to me my brother and three other guys said we were going to jail for selling them drugs, in front of his house.

He said I was going first and it happened, just like that. I was just thinking about how my dad just told me. Eventually, I had to call so they wouldn't think I was missing. My mother answered the phone and she said she was going to get me out. I got out on a personal bond, this time. Later on in the fall, I met a women and she was 12yrs older than me. You knew that was right my alley. We were cool at first, until we had sex. I had to put it down. We saw one another, for a while. One night went out to City Blue to buy some clothes and was thinking of doing all night flights, while selling drugs. I went to the liquor store and my night was set. I had just made $1000 and my father told me I should stay in the house. I said I needed another $1000. He told me again don't go back out there. I wish I would've listened. This certain person picked me up and he was an informant and I didn't know it. He came to the block and picked me and said his people wanted some dope. He was selling weed, but it was a trap. I got in the car and we went and got some girls and liquor. We met the dude and it was funny, because the man didn't want it. The guy I was with went into the store and he was on my phone asking some people we know do they want some weed.

I heard this clear that they didn't want weed. I had cocaine on me and we were driving to people I didn't know to sell drugs. Once we arrived to the street 134th and Bell, they were outside. I got out the car and let them hit the blunt and talk. All of a sudden, Cleveland Vice Police came out of know where. I hopped back in the car and they came straight for me. I was set up. I was scrambling, with the crack. I was trying to find a place to put it. It was inside my pants. When I got out the car the crack fell down my leg and onto the officer's boot. They hit the jackpot. I knew it was over and the only place I was going was to jail that night. As I was riding downtown to the city jail, the officer said he knew I had something else. He knew about the weed I had. While I was in jail, I didn't want to call home, because I knew my father was going to answer and say I told you. I called and couldn't get through, so my friend told my parents. While in there for 3 days, someone stole over $5000 from me. My dudes paid my bond to get me out and I told them I would pay them back in two days. I had 3 different bonds and it was crazy. I was going back and forth to court. I was working my job, but it got worse. They were trying to give me 18 months, in jail. I told then no and kept switching lawyers.

From The Street To The Pulpit

I went to court 18 times spent like $17,000 on my case and they gave me rehab, probation and house arrest. In 2003, they put me at the Self Center rehab place on east 55th. They told me to turn myself in for about 30 days. I had to have a smoke out before I went, in here. We gathered at my cousin house and I set out a half pound of weed. We tried to smoke the whole thing. The next day, I was riding down to the rehab center smoking like it was nothing. I arrived, with my clothes with me. I was going to be there for the next 3 months. I had to get my mind set, on this spot. When I got there, they gave me the run down about the place rules and regulations. I went to my bed and saw some people I knew and met some new folks. While I was in there, God was speaking to me. I still wasn't listening what He was saying. We had got 3 meals a day, sometimes good and sometimes bad. I was a jokester and always making people laugh. I got cool with a lot of folks, in there. The day before I got out, I told the place I had to work. They wanted to call my job, so I gave them a friend's number. He answered told and them I had to work and let me out. On my way to the bus stop, some guys tried to jump me at about 4:30am. I went to the hood to see my girl. We were going through ups and downs.

I had to get her right and she was cool. The halfway house called my friend back and he didn't answer. It was time for me to go back down there and I was drinking and hoping they breathe machine wouldn't go off. That Monday I had to report to my probation officer, to put me on house arrest. While on house arrest, I went back to my old ways selling dope, at the job and the house. My mom and dad would have killed me. I was still working, but not enough money. I'm telling you God was with me. Later in this year, I got off house arrest. I wasn't listening to the probation officer. It was the last month of the year 2003 and I got bad news. Both of my good friends died a week apart. My life was really in pieces. My dude Big C and my best friend T-Lo got killed. I was ready to go to war with whom ever. The devil had all of my mind. I did not know God was still holding me down. I was still not listening to what God was calling me to. I had caught another case, on Memorial Day weekend. I was in the bus stop by Tower City waiting on the bus, with drugs all on me. I was rolling up a blunt, but didn't know an undercover cop was next to me the whole time. When I finished rolling the blunt, I saw a car coming my way and didn't know it was vice cops.

I started to run and the guy next to me grabbed my neck and said he was Cleveland Police. I was sick. I was on my way back to this dirty city jail. I got caught with five rocks of cocaine and an ounce of weed. I told the judge I was smoking crack to get out of the case. It wasn't going to work out the way I thought. I was let out on a bond and went on the run. I didn't go back to court, so they started looking for me and I was hiding high and low. I was tired of running, but didn't want to go back to jail. I was still in the relationship with the older woman and it was driving me nuts. I felt like I was in love with her, but I knew she was cheating on me. I was not married to the woman. I just lived there. She had me gone. As I am writing this book, I just remember all this stuff the devil tried to do to kill me. He had a mean strong hold on me. I was going to church and getting prophesied to, but was not listening to what God was saying to me. We all fall into this trap of the enemy. I had started to go to club MODA and started meeting celebrities and making myself hotter, in these streets. On January 26, 2005, I was enjoying my birthday. I was having a good time, but was also planning my funeral. I told my mom to put me in an all-white suit and get two churches, because that's how many people I knew in these streets.

I knew out of town drug dealers, too. I told her and my auntie. I was still running from the police and acting crazier now, because I was smoking PCP more and popping ecstasy pills. My life was going down the drain. The winter was over and now it was spring and the police were still trying to catch up with me. I started selling drugs in a different neighborhood and took over a crack house down on fleet Ave. These guys down here didn't like me, but so what. Me and my hood friends went down there with guns and took over. My dudes told me don't do it, but you know I didn't listen. I was being hard headed. We were now on a high speed chase, from the police. We had guns, drugs, etc. I drove up to 130th and Kinsman, down to 126th to 124th Union and all the way across to Corlett. We throwing stuff out the car the whole time. I lost them and ran into a brick wall. The air bag in the car didn't come out, but the passengers did. I couldn't feel my legs. I told my dudes to get out the car and run I would take the case. They left me and I got my legs together and crawled out and started to run. I looked back at the car and knew it was nothing but God, because the car was totaled. One of my friends had broken his shoulder and the other had broken his glasses, but we all got away.

They called me on grand theft auto. I couldn't get caught, because I was still on the run. It was summer and the police planned good to get me. This is how the day went. I was getting ready for the rap group to go to the radio station and had gotten cd's and everything. This was my rap group that I was managing at the time RSC. I was walking down the street and sold to the old man across the street. I sold him some weed and walked back across the street to my mom's house. The police came about 10 cars deep with detectives and everything. I only had some black and mild's swisher sweets and seven bags of weed. I laughed and slammed my phone down to the ground, so they couldn't get evidence. The police didn't even put the handcuffs on me. They took me down to the station and started giving each other high fives, like the caught a king pin or something. They put me in a cell for about 45 minutes. One of the officers came to the cell and said they needed to talk to me. He said whatever I wanted to sell they could provide me with it and started naming people from the neighborhood and wanted me to set people up. I told them I don't talk to police. I said I wanted a lawyer and they needed to leave me alone.

The next day they woke me up and told me the head of narcotics wanted me. I told him I didn't know anything and I was waiting on the other district to come get me. They did have pictures of me, but not selling drugs. Cleveland police finally came and got me and took me to the city county jail.

Chapter Eight

God was Speaking

While in jail for the last time, I saw my little cousin in here, with me. I told him I was only going to be here for a couple of days. While I was in there, I went to bible study and met a guard who was a preacher. I knew the scriptures me and the preacher told me I didn't belong in there. He said, "I see God all in you." It blew my mind. The next day my cousin was going to court and I was just waiting on God. That night God showed me a dream of me and my cousin getting out and it was a bright sunny day. My cousin had the same dream. It was real. They called both of our names. I couldn't believe it. God got us out for a reason, because his father was about to die. The next couple of months after his father died, we were all shocked. I remember being at the hospital in the bath room and I heard God say he was gone. The door opened in the bathroom and no one was there. This really freaked me out and that's when I knew God spoke to me. RIP E Love uncle Earl. I had to go back to court and the judge said if you come back down here, you will get five years. They put me in AA meetings and I was going to drug classes. I was cool with that.

I wanted a new girlfriend, so my brother baby mama hooked me up with this EC girl. She looked good, but had a son. I had love for her, but wasn't in love with her. We would drink a lot and I was popping ecstasy pills, like I lost my mind. I would pick her up on Friday and she would stay till Sunday. I had started to like her a lot and she didn't know it, because she has always been played by men. It was the end of 2005 and cold outside, when we heard a knock at the door. It was my uncle Joseph, looking very sick. He only had one pair of clothes and needed us to help him. We took him in and he started to get back on track and got saved and filled with the Holy Ghost. I had got saved and filled with the Holy Ghost too. We had lived together. God was blessing us with apartment, van and food stamps, but that was all we had. The landlord was so nice to furnish our whole house and things were going good. I didn't know my uncle was real sick. He had west Nile virus and HIV. I still loved him regardless what he had. I remember he used to go to church praising god and running around the church like there was no tomorrow. He told me that God let him live a little longer for me. I just cried that day, because of how God thought about me, to let him live.

From The Street To The Pulpit

The month had passed and now in February of 2006, my first cousin Andrea we called "DREA" got murdered. It was a sad day. My cousin got stabbed about 55 times, in front of her kids. Her son told the police who the guy was and what happened. The guy had took her car. It had made the news here, in Cleveland and surrounding areas. Our family had lost a great family member. She was truly loved, RIP Andrea Brown. The day of the home going I had to be prepared to speak my first time. God gave me the words to say. I saw people just listening and didn't know I touched so many lives, at that moment. God was preparing me for greatness and I didn't even know it. So many people came to God on this day. My uncle was at a cross roads, with life. The doctors called me and said we need to meet you. We would have to put him in Hospice. I started to cry, because there were so many plans, goals and things we were supposed to do together. God had better plans for him. I remember his last words, before he went incoherent that he was going to be alright. It was about 5:30am, when I got the call that he had passed away. The word God gave me was harsh for the family, but I just had to deliver the word from God. My family has a lot of gifts from God. God was filling me with words to say.

I showed my mom the stuff that God gave me to say. God gave it I am going to say it. I got to the funeral and said what thus said the Lord. After the funeral some, of my family members didn't talk to me anymore. This is life. I had taken a long drive after words and wherever the car took me I was going to go. I ended up in Canton, Ohio and knew some folks down there. They embraced me and took in and we talked laughed and I came back to Cleveland. As the summer came I had job and bought a car. I had an apartment too and started hanging back with old friends and doing bad things. I was going to the bar not drinking, but buying everybody drinks and they would buy me red bulls. I should have known that this was not good and the devil was winning me back. I had people saying drink a little bit. It won't hurt. So, I started with a little wine and then black and mild's. I started thinking God forgot about me. I had a good job working at a toy factory. I was working and focusing on the goals that I had for myself in life. I was going backwards, in life once again. I went to work one day and started smoking weed and got injured and almost lost my hand. I went to the bathroom to try to stop the bleeding and I wouldn't stop.

I just had got hired through the company and knew if they did drug test me, I was going to be fired. They sent me to the hospital and you know I failed the drug test and they had let me go. I had went back to what I know selling pills, weed, and cocaine. I had started popping ecstasy real bad. I had the women always around me and we would go to after hour joints, strip clubs, etc. I took selling drugs more serious this time. The thirst for the money was real too. I took it to heart as of earlier in my life it was just a game and now I was the game. I had got another job working as a temp and they about to hire me. I was sleeping with two or three women, at one time in a night. The more money I made the more stuff I started to do. 2007 was here and I was really partying, having sex and selling drugs. I had gone to a bar one night and the guys I was getting my drugs from was an informant and I didn't know. The guys locked us in seven against two and we didn't back down. I was just saying I just can't hit the ground. Two of the guys had got my brother in the bathroom and I was fighting five of them. All I knew was one guy hit me with the bar stool and split my forehead wide open. I hit the floor and bounced back up and they ran. They had to rush me to the hospital and I was bleeding so bad nothing could stop it.

From The Street To The Pulpit

They told my brother I was not going to make it. He was crying really bad. I told him to stay strong and I was going to be alright. I said a prayer and closed my eyes. I knew I was not going to heaven, if I had died. This man appeared and sewed me up. I had three layers of stitches, plus thirty going down. I was going to have another war wound, for life. I came out the hospital and my brother was so happy. God knew he had a better plan for me and didn't let me find these guys that assaulted me. After this, I started hanging out with all women. My best friend was a women and so cool. She had five kids and always nice to people. She was letting me sleep with her friends and she was setting me up with. The year going good. Also in this year, I had got shot at and someone called my mother and they had me, in the trunk of their car. They first shot at my brother and then called my cousin and said they were going to kill him. The end of 2007 I had met this special women and I lied to her, from the top. She was a nice young lady and could cook too. I never really had that. I always had dope girls who wanted my money. This girl didn't know I sold drugs or anything about me. It even got to the point where she was taking me to work, all the time.

From The Street To The Pulpit

I had started feeling her but I wasn't doing right. I was trying to have her and eat my cake to. I knew it was wrong, because she was too cool. We started hanging tuff. I would sell drugs all day and come home to her, late at night. We had moved to this house on Parkview. I was liking her a lot and never had love like this. I thought it was the food. They say way to a man's heart is food. She would leave the door open for me and I could come in, anytime of the night. This was like heaven. I was selling drugs right up under nose and she didn't find out. I had started going to this club called the castle on the Westside. This place was my new kick it spot and I started to know people and the security guards. My best friend and I started selling pills real heavy. We also used them too, real heavy. One night my best friend had gotten some pills not from our normal connection. I told them to meet me at the castle and we were going to have a good time. I had popped a pill at 12:45am and after thirty minutes didn't feel the effect, so I was about to do another one. This is the first time I listened to my mind and I didn't do another one. My best friend called me and said the pills were weak. I called my best friend and said they won't let me in and I would see her tomorrow.

I was so high off that one pill that I couldn't move. My friend had to drive me home and I was only asleep about an hour, when the phone rang. I was told my best friend had passed. I started throwing up and couldn't believe this. I got up and didn't believe it and went to her house. I called my brother and we cried all day. The next day police come and get me and started questioning me about what happened. The word on the street was I sold her the pills and I was the pill man. I told them I needed to see a lawyer. They trying to get me for murder. They let me go and said they would be back. She had left behind five kids. I was so sad. They funeral day was here and I didn't know what I was going to do, when I saw her in the casket. I was so hurt and cried the whole time. I had words to say, but they didn't let anyone speak. I said I wasn't touching no pills any more. I went home to my girlfriend and just cried. About six months passed and I went to court, but beat the case.

Chapter Nine

Family Life

I started thinking about life and doing the family thing. I was really ready to change my life, at this point. I hadn't been out in a while. I was just thinking in my mind that when this last couple of ounces of Kush weed was gone, I am done with the drug game. It was my birthday and I wanted to party, one more time. I bought a gallon of liquor and we were drunk, before we went to the party. We got to the club and bought more liquor and Moet bottles. I was ready to smoke now and I was feeling myself. I went to the bathroom and my dude was working in there and I paid him to smoke. I came out the bathroom and these guys started to stare at me. I was by the speaker and dancing my song came on take your shirt off, by Gucci Man. As I was in there, I heard the voice, of my bishop speaking to me. It freaked me out and I could hear the prophecies he told me, since 1999. I got scared and told my brother I heard the bishop. While this was going on, one the guys that was staring showed me a gun and told me I was a dead man at me and said you are a dead man.

I had told God if you get me out of this, I promise I never leave the church. I got home and was so happy that God gave me another chance. The next two months I was going to church and my girlfriend started to come to with her kids. It was Sunday, December 19, 2008 and I was at church and my brother told his testimony of how our friends was dying and how God been dealing with him. The church had called an altar call and I was the first one up there ready for God to clean me up and restore my soul. I was on there for like three hours and they were casting out so many spirits. I had so many it was like I was bleeding out my soul. God was purging me. In January 2009, I was about to propose to my girlfriend. I didn't have a ring, but God spoke to my auntie to give me one that she never wore. I went over her house and she said God told her to give me and this it blew my mind, because I didn't tell her I wanted to marry this girl. The ring still had the tag on it and it was a $5000 ring. God spoke to me and said this is a gift. I went home and asked my soon to be wife if she would marry me? I was not romantic, because I was still a little hood. She said yes! We were planning for the wedding. I went to church and told my bishop and he said did you ask God if this was your wife. I went home and prayed and ask god.

God didn't give me an answer for about 3 months. He gave me the answer and I told the bishop and now we were going to counseling. The month of May came and we got baptized together. I asked God, when I came up to have me speaking in an unknown tongue. He answered my prayer. The next couple of months came we were about to have a double wedding. My sister and I were having a wedding together and I was in training to be a minister. September 5, 2009, was the wedding day. I was so happy everything going well and about 300 people were at this wedding. I was shocked. It was standing room only. I was so happy that God changed me and I had a family. My wife is the best thing that has happened to me. We had so much fun on this day. Life was going good and changes in my life were, for the good. Years go by and now I about to have my trial sermon, before I get my minister's license. October 2013, I preached my first sermon "SOMETHING GOOD IS COMING OUT OF THIS". I had gone on a fast for about a month and God gave me this message. I had preached messages before, just so the Bishop could show me what I had to tighten up on. This message I got in bold letters and knew I was called by God.

I was called back in 1999, but ran from my calling. The Bible says in Hebrews 12:6, "For whom the Lord loveth He chaseteneth, and scourgeth every son who He recieveth. I am leaving you all and telling you God can change you and help you with any situation, in your life. Just believe in Him. He is the only source you have. This book is one of the many God going to get the glory from. In the next book, I will talk about marriage, so get ready for it. I pray that you enjoyed this journey of my life. I really want to thank my family for backing me up, through my process.

Made in United States
Orlando, FL
28 June 2024